Dedication to my Ancestors and Spirit Guides

@Gloria Sarker, South Australia, May 2022
eMotion- Affirmative Poem-Part 1

ISBN **978-0-6454016-0-8**

Contents

Hope

Hope!
I have a telescope.
lots in the sky
starts at nights.

I hold onto my wish and
learn appreciation.
The collective mourns,
teaching us compassion.

We are here
for a reason.
Love and peace
please!
Don't miss
your gift.

Forgive us
mother Earth.
give us another chance.

Color

RGB - Red, Green and Blue
are the Primary Clue.
absence of color is Black,
all color needs it
to make more color.

Green is the color of life,
dark-green, yellow-green
olive-green means more meaning.

BDS - Black Dog Syndrome
big black dogs need chains
to control.

Black People need
training and correction.
prison and addiction
genocide and rape
blood and gene
beyond you think.

Time for
spiritual awakening.

Why are you fearful of
people with colorful?

Peace and forgiveness
take time to build trust.

Nest

You make your

little nest
to sit and rest.

You think
it is the best.
not knowing how
to escape.

Why are you complaining?
you want to see the world
before your
last breath.

You made your nest!
want to break it?
Put up your head
see the world
in front of your face.

Ceremony

Incense in the morning
enjoy your service
precious gift
nice smoky smell.

Fresh new days
thank you, my friend TanTan,
stay there lifelong.
grateful to have you.
friends are valuable.

Pair

Many have pairs
eyes and ears
kindness and care

A few are different
like politicians and lawyers
elites and institutions
flood and harvest
summer and sex.

Others are
co-dependence and narcissistic
vampire and empath
ego and pride.

Trauma and healing
money and bills

Funny ones
anger and cancer
fear and anxiety

Autoimmune
and true to yourself

You have a pair
that exists in reality
inside your duality.
focus on the divine unity.

Curiosity

What is this?
little piece!
first sight
check and bite.

No No No
don't trust.
it's a trap.

Fear?
have seen this ever
don't go near.

Brave enough
taste yum.
waste my time
fight inside.

Do it or don't do it
have the courage
to be curious.

Little Girl

Sweet talker Suzi
drug addict
drug dealer
sleeps with many men.

Little girl's last place
to live was unsafe.

Abundant by parents
mental illness
drugs and domestic violence.

Little girl was the carer
of her young siblings.
now she cares for Suzi's
two autistic boys.

Little girl was dirty
smelled bad
confused about her sexuality.

What does she tell us?

Poor girl finds a safe place
to live in Suzi's house.

Image

You have two images
twice a day.
dusk and dawn
bright sun
rises and sets.

You realise
your time has come.
no more being left behind,
enjoy your
everyday life.

Ego Supremacy

I am better than you,
how dare
you compare!

You're green
I am red,
I bet
I am the best.

Who cares?
does it matter?
I'd rather say
I am better.

Self talk

Adult: I raise my child better than my parents did.
Inner Child: Sounds good, you should.
Adult: Neglect and abuse has no excuse.
Inner Child: Great parenting! Do you listen your child?
Adult: Love and care, I always share.
Inner Child: My tantrums make you yell.
Adult: Can you stop? I ask for expert help.
Inner Child: Quiet your mind, there's a hole in your soul.
Adult: Soul is bullshit, no science behind this.
Inner Child: You repeat until you do it.
Adult: Tell me how to learn and heal?
Inner Child: Let's grow, you and I.
Adult: It's hard. Change mind. My parents are best forever.
Adult: Don't care of threat and fear.
Inner Child: I can gear play and cheers.

New Way

Evidence and references,
journal or peer reviewed
views are void or validation.

Make it your way
they can go via the highway.

Perception and mistakes
grammar or systems
institutions and schools.

Power and mind control.
are you vulnerable?
your way or our way?
East or West?
Middle East?
Indigenous?
they exist.

Why listen to ancestors?
faith and trust,
secret knowledge and peace,
they survived for thousands of years.
does your mind is playing this year?

Comparison

There is always someone
worse than you.
you give
you serve
you deserve
and you disappear.

There is always someone
better than you.
you receive
you manifest
you fly
and you fall.

There is always equality.
balance and harmony.
enjoy and embrace
the journey
the light and the love.

Perfection is Illusion

Make an appointment
with your disappointments.

All your sadness
needs some forgiveness.

Find your strength
rest and test
you can do your best.

Pour a bit of love
for you and other.

Pain and hurt
is an addiction.
time for fun
and seduction.

It will pass

It's a thought
only a thought.

It's a memory
just a memory.

My attachment and
addiction
to my memories.

My pain
my sorrow
that's my expectation.

No judgement
stay still.

Here come new thoughts
new preferences!
observe with no reaction.
It will pass.
Stay focused on the LOVE.

Walk in the Hills

She was in the hills
in the bush
by herself.

Walking and wondering
watching and talking to
birds, trees and animals.

The smells of plants, the cool breeze.
no GPS worked there
no old paths
lost in the hills.

But she listened and kept walking.

Worried and despairing
no joy and then she falls.
stuck in pain.

She kept going
one foot at a time.
she enjoyed her alone time
she kept walking
she kept trying.

Suddenly across the bottom
of a mountain,
she found a way.
a tiny little kangaroo path.
she smiled
she was brave
she listened to herself.

Promise

I promise I will be with you always.
Your worries
insecurities
hurts
anger
no matter, I will be with you always,
my little one!

Your tantrums
swearing
yelling
kicking
I promise I will never leave you alone.
you are wanted
you are special
you are loved.

I promise I will bring joy,
love and compassion to you.
I will listen to you,
be with you in grief and sadness.
I promise I will be with you on your fun days,
in adventures and happy days,
in victorious and relaxing days!

I promise I will be more patient,
my little one,
more calm and connected.
I promise I will shift my focus to do my best for you.
I promise I will protect you in your days of fight and fear.
my secure connection will help you to conquer the world.
I promise I will try to help you to help myself.
I promise to learn from you.

I promise to encourage you
honour you
respect you.
I promise I will wash away your tears.
Guilt!
Shame!
I promise I will always be with you.
you matter to me,
my little one!

Womb Manifestation

I will manifest you,
my unborn little one.
my singlehood will shine
my womanhood will be praised.

I will call you Love
No one is allowed to call you Fetus.
You are made wonderfully
fairly and lovingly.

Your light will sparkle
your presence will shine
your hands will heal souls
you will speak before it happens.

You will forgive
you will command
you will bring joy to humanity,
my little light!
No more suffering
no more tears
the best will play with you.
harmony re-established
helps arrives before you ask
honesty and peace have been established,
my little one!

You will come into my womb
I try to give you the best world.
you are powerful.
I know you will make it.
you choose to come into my womb,
my little one!

Prophet & Prostitute

Then the prophet Hosea said,
that prostitute!
do I have to love her?
marry her?
she belongs to all.
rare to trust
my shame!
she is beautiful,
but not faithful.
yes, she left me again.
that prostitute!

Love and grace.
how many times can I say 'yes'?
she left me again.
she is pregnant.
whose child is that?
I say 'yes'.
raise all children.
she left again.

In the dark night on the street,
I pay her to bring home.
she believes my love is fake.

I know it will never end.
Gomer, the name of that prostitute
is my home that I choose.

Little boy and Cave People

Little boy
playing in the woods
dancing and singing
finds a cave in the forest.

He walks down into the cave.
he listens to
whispers!
down! further down!

Deep inside in the dark cave
he smells… people?
deep in the cave.

He says there is light
outside the cave.
big sun, lovely moon,
beautiful birds, plants
and cool breezes.
come!
come with me.
I show you the light.

No one believes him,
they're scared and untrusting.
A few, very few, young little ones
follow him.
Holding hands, holding each other in the dark,
step by step, slowly
they come out into the light.

Alice in wonderland!
A beautiful place to live.

peace and harmony,
new Earth.
little boy plays in the woods
saved and safe.
take time to build trust.

Empty Grave

Why you weeping
at my grave,
mourning and crying?
I am not there.
why you leaving flowers
on my empty tomb?
I am not there.

I am at home
where I came from.

You can be brave
not afraid of death
don't cry about your deeds,
things that you missed
wanted to finish.

When it's time to leave
I'll meet you there,
where we all share
spirit and light.

Enjoy your life
in body and mind
earthly delights.

I Am

I am who I choose to become
I am who I am.
walk away from chaos
to peace and quiet.
no shame!
I've walked a long way
to become
who I am.

I am here
where I'm meant to be!
I share space and time,
learn so much and
wisdom shows as I grow.

I am who I am
sharing and caring
I am the loved one.
My past is gone,
what remains?
the precious present.

I don't complain,
it's a compliment.
each day
I am who
I choose to become.

Triggers

Some silly young boys say,
"Tiger! Tiger!"
I say, "Trigger! Trigger!"
Intense emotions
fear and projection
all the destruction
reaction and protection
makes them bigger and bigger –
I name it "Trigger".

Tiger has a rapid response,

doesn't need a reminder.
How dare you, Trigger!
I am a mighty Tiger.

Quantum mechanics
optics and lights
not knowing how to shine.
Let's walk through the dark nights.

Who controls me?
My power?
My wounds?

Sit with the wound.
I want to feel.
Mature beings
are willing to heal.

When Triggers come,
some silly boys say,
"Triggers! Triggers!"
I say, "Tiger! Tiger!"

Option

You have an option,
you know your worth.
you have a voice.
A crown!
You are the Queen.

King has a Kingdom,
Serve people and land;
poor to rich
freedom and comfort.

You have a life,
wise and confident.
You know you are the best,
selfless and self-worth.

You have a heart.
Standards.
Empowered!
You are the Queen.

Love Focus Society

Not long ago
only hundreds of years
beautiful human beings
lived on this earth.

We didn't have to buy
air and water
rain and fountains
fishing or home-grown food.

There was a time
friendly people met in
the local shops for
coffee and tea,
shared life and laughter.

There was a time
we didn't have to pay for vehicles
or build our homes
get married or protest.

There was a time
we didn't need to go court;
we honoured the local elders
and lived in harmony.

There was a time
we didn't have to buy news;
there was a time
we didn't have to sell ourselves.

There was a time

you listened to yourself.
There was a time
you gave away your power
to the wicked world.

Now is the time:
bring back your stolen power
you are powerful
human beings.

Not Too Shy

Don't be shy
if you have nothing.
Why cry?

Don't be shy!
Go for a long ride
under the sky
on a quiet night.

Don't mind
if you hide.
Missed and ignored
mingle in the crowd
overlooked,
please shout mild!
If you are the middle child.

Don't be shy,
scream high!
Make your own space.
Raise your hand
and say again,
"Don't you dare
push me away.
I never give up."

Don't be shy
Neck on the first night.
Don't miss the kiss!
Make a date for yourself
under the full moon.
You are cool.

Don't be shy –
walk an extra mile.
Don't be shy,
snore at midnight.
Don't be shy.
Fly high in the sky.

Poetry Competition

That little girl
was happy,
happy enough to dance by herself
singing, jumping and bumping.
Everyone was amused.
Daddy says, "My little one!
My joy and happiness!
She pleases me."

That little girl
was nervous and stuttering,
delayed in development.
Mum says, "I will raise you differently,
freely and independently,
teach you secrets of love,
race, sex and gender.
Remember, love is your highest priority".

That little girl is confused
gender and sex
policy and practices
real and fake.

That little girl works in a place where
she tries many times
in difficult situations.
No chance for promotion
needs more skills
as English is the second language
black woman
needs to run many more miles.

Mum says, "Forget and forgive,
keep love as your priority."
That little girl writes poems
to be published,
hopes to win the competition.

Little girl is worried.
Who will be the judges?
Is English their second language?
What race and color ?
There is no response.
Don't see many blacks.
The other place calls them Soul Lounge.
Says "We do poems in our ways,
Come!
You belong here,
we're all second class."

Daddy says, "No competition!
It opens the door to deception.
Love all.
Let all souls shine.
Blessed are them who listen to their parents.
Love and light,
you are my child."

Delilah's Deception

Then Samson said loudly
"Almighty God!
Give my power back
one more time!

They are joking
and mocking me!
I am suffering,
my shame!
I am in pain.

Give me strength.
I repent!
I trust her,
that lady Delilah.

I was foolish.
I was in love.
She tests me many times,
she's a liar and greedy.
I told her my secrets –
my strength.
My power.
I tell you now
what I learnt.

Leave them
who betray you first.
Watch what they do
not what they say.
Sweet mouth
and slippery tongue
never make
things right.

Now I pray
as they feast,
blind and failing
in the jail.

I push the walls.
God gives me strength
one last time.
My heart is at peace.
I repent!
Finally, I have done it.

People come into our life
enemies and friends
to teach us a lesson.
Trust yourself
and avoid the pain.
It's your strength.

One Day

One day
after many long days

yes, one day
we will meet again.
We'll see each other again.
and sit in a quiet place.
One day,
I hope!

On that day,
we will explain
what happened.
We will tell each other
what really distanced us.
We will finally understand.
All questions will be answered.
One day we will be more mature,
for sure!
We will see how it worked for us.
We will see our past better.

Today we can not
return into our past.
Now, in this moment,
I can rewrite my future.
This day
will become my past.

That future me
will give thanks for my past days

that showed me how to live,
how to love.

Until then I leave you behind.
Until then I will live my life.
Until then I say good bye.

One day you will ask me,
why did you hide?
One day I will realise,
why did I fight?
One day I will know,
why did I cry?

One day we will meet in peace.
Until then, I let you go.
It's not meant to be.

Let me go. I wish you the best.
One day we will talk.

The Mirror

When I want to throw it away
I find there is no way.
No motivation.
No inspiration.
Life takes its own path.
I find no way.

I return to my vicious cycle
troubling my body and mind.
I call it illness –
my physical and mental disturbance.
I return to me.
There is no way to leave.

When I want to be well
it runs away from me.
I try hard -
I cry in fear.
Why are you taking away
what is dear?

I say my prayer.
Nothing happens.
I can't make my way.
Life takes its own way.

I sit on my grave
take my last breath
it's not fair.

What have I done?
Only mirror!

Funny Tummy

Funny feelings in my tummy
Can't tell my mummy
Funny tummy!

My mind is busy
Please let my body rest.
I want to be perfect.

Long list to achieve
all done on time
I want to accomplish
a tick on each task.

Marks on my tummy
I create my pain
with my impatience
Undone tasks
hard work
not knowing how to relax.

I am fearful
I am scared
I can not let go of the past.

Who can help me
heal the pain
in my funny tummy?
I wait a while,
believe I am safe.
Happy tummy
settles at the end.

Shift Work

Night shift
way too long!

Long eight hours
in the homeless shelter
All are asleep
Only me doing the shift.

Doing my duties and tasks
Fuck!
Life sucks!

My body and mind
I am not kind to them
Funny tummy
Sleep apnea
Snoring
Teeth grinding
Difficulty breathing
Deprivation of my needs
Declining health
Brings inflammation.
I am no one
When did you see me in daytime?

Night shift
pays my bills.
Few more hours to go.
How long do I have to do this shit?

Anxiety

Let go of anxiety
Let go of fear
and poverty.

Let go of negative self-talk
Let go of false beliefs.

I would like to feel.
How about I feel?
How does it feel to have abundance?
To be prosperous?
To be fearless?
To be free?

I feel how it feels to be loved
How do I love?
How do I live that life I want?

I start to love myself
my thoughts turn into
grace, kindness, gratitude and love.

I forgive my past and all my hurts.
I forgive myself.
I am blessed.
My wisdom and light
guides me.
Everyday
I overcome my fear
my anxiety.
Every day
Every hour
Every minute!

Made in the USA
Monee, IL
07 July 2026

56552172R00024